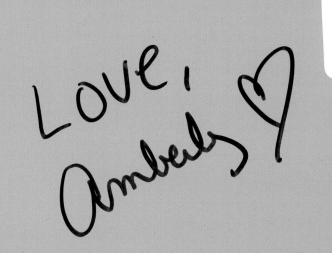

Love,
Amberly ♡

The
BIRTHDAY
Balloon Fairy

If you're like me, you wait all year to see if The Birthday Balloon Fairy will appear.

Have I shown what it means to turn my next age?

Or do I have more to prove at this stage?

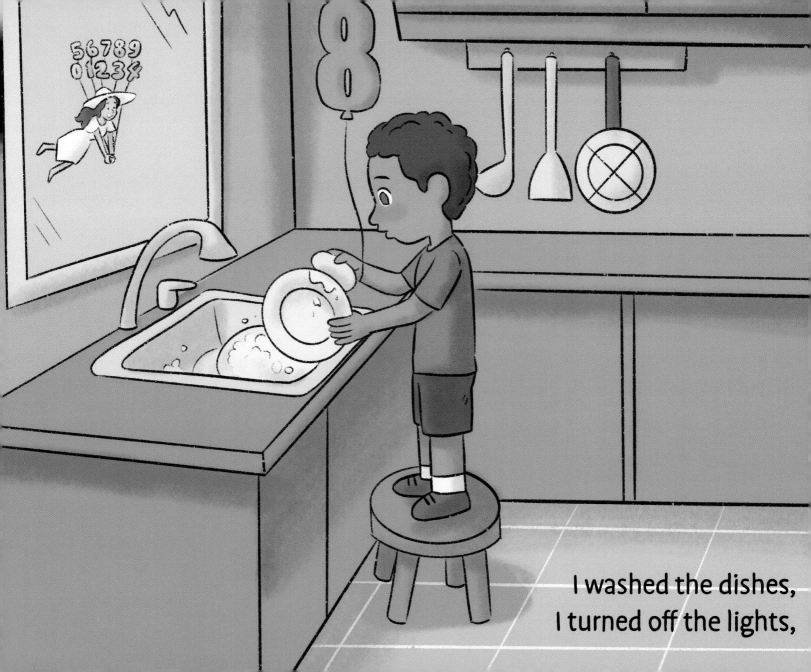

I washed the dishes,
I turned off the lights,

I even went to sleep in my own bed every night.

Sure, there was a time or two when I whined or complained and—well we won't talk about that time with the glue.

Now that my birthday is soon, will I get my new balloon?

Tonight's the night. I must turn off the light, to see if The Birthday Balloon Fairy will take flight.

So when I'm told it's time for bed,
I say a prayer and drift off
to somewhere.

When I wake, it is tough to believe...I do in fact feel taller than on my Birthday Eve.

I'll spare you each line. But please know when it's your time, The Birthday Balloon Fairy will use all her magic to deliver your wish during the nighttime.

You'll continue learning and growing

and how fast it goes will be mind-blowing.

So keep being kind and trying your best.

And may I suggest, look for signs that The Birthday Balloon Fairy is near as it gets close to your time of the year.

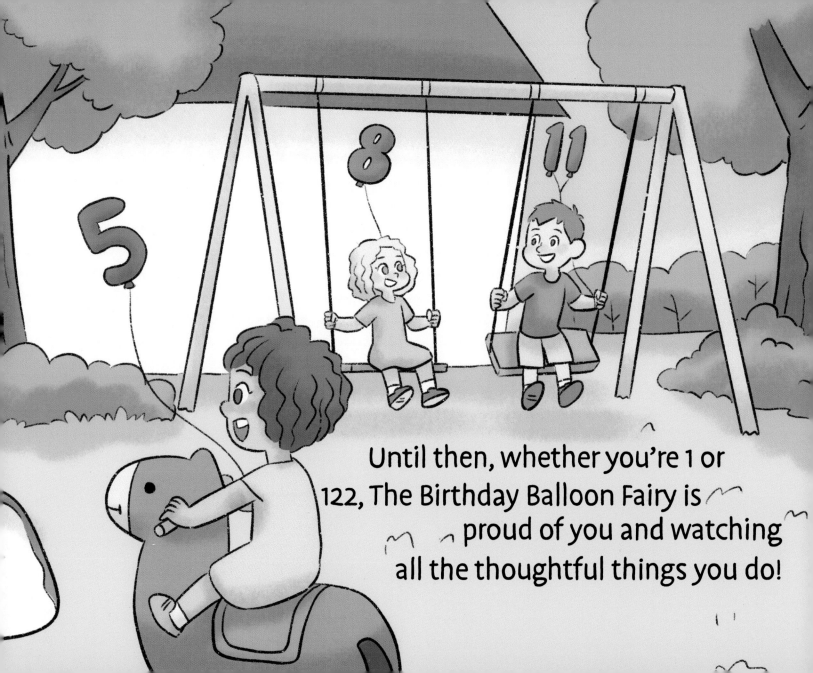

Until then, whether you're 1 or 122, The Birthday Balloon Fairy is proud of you and watching all the thoughtful things you do!